Valentine's Day
DOT MARKERS
ACTIVITY BOOK

35 Valentine's Day Illustrations to color with Dot Markers

THIS BOOK BELONGS TO

TIPS

1. Position a piece of paper or cardboard under the page to avoid bleed-through

2. You can cut each page along the dotted line on the back and hang them where you want

KINDRELL
Land Press

DISCOVER ALL OUR BOOKS

Scan this QR code to find them

Our dot markers books collection

FOR ALL YEAR

Dinosaurs
Unicorns
Vehicles
Sea & Ocean Life
Animals ABC 123

FOR THE HOLIDAYS

Valentine's Day
Easter
Mother's Day
4th of July

Summer
Thanksgiving
Halloween ABC 123
Christmas

Christmas ABC 123
Hanukkah ABC 123
...and more to come!

Get ready for Easter with our book!

CUPID

BEAR
IN LOVE

BOX OF CHOCOLATES

CUPCAKE

VALENTINE'S DAY CARD

KITTY

HEARTS

CANDY

LOVE

LOVE LETTER

CUTE BUNNY

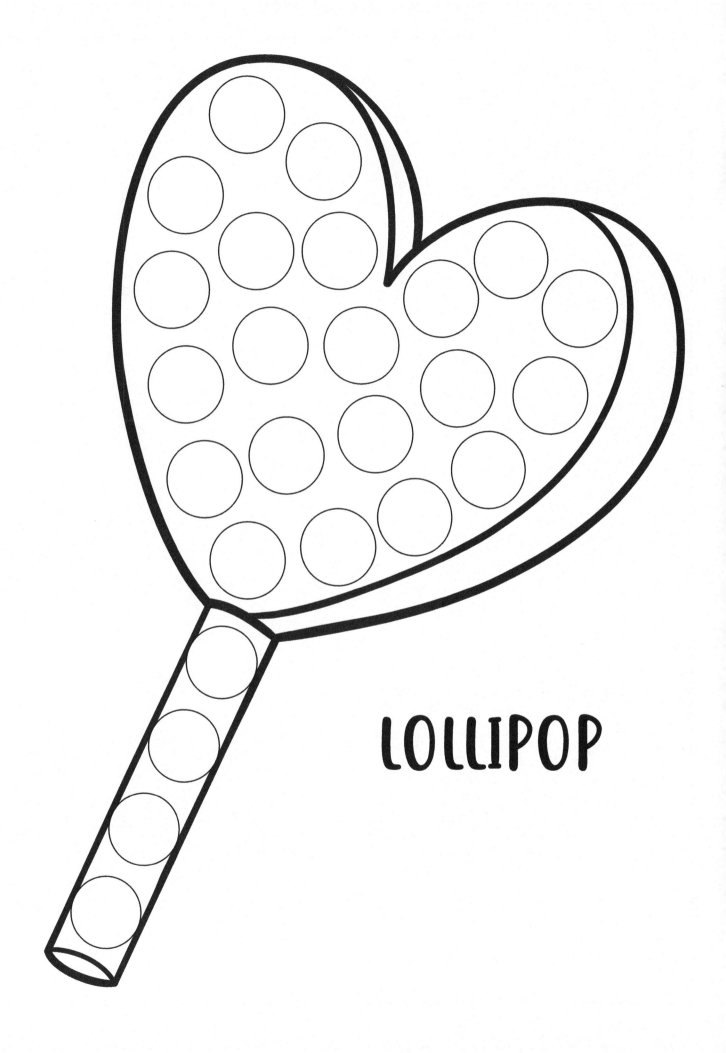

LOLLIPOP

FLOWERS

HEART LOCK

BEE

SWEETHEARTS

DAISY

DIAMOND RING

UNICORN

DOG

DOVE

TEDDY BEAR

CHOCOLATE BAR

SERENADE

CAKE

PRESENT

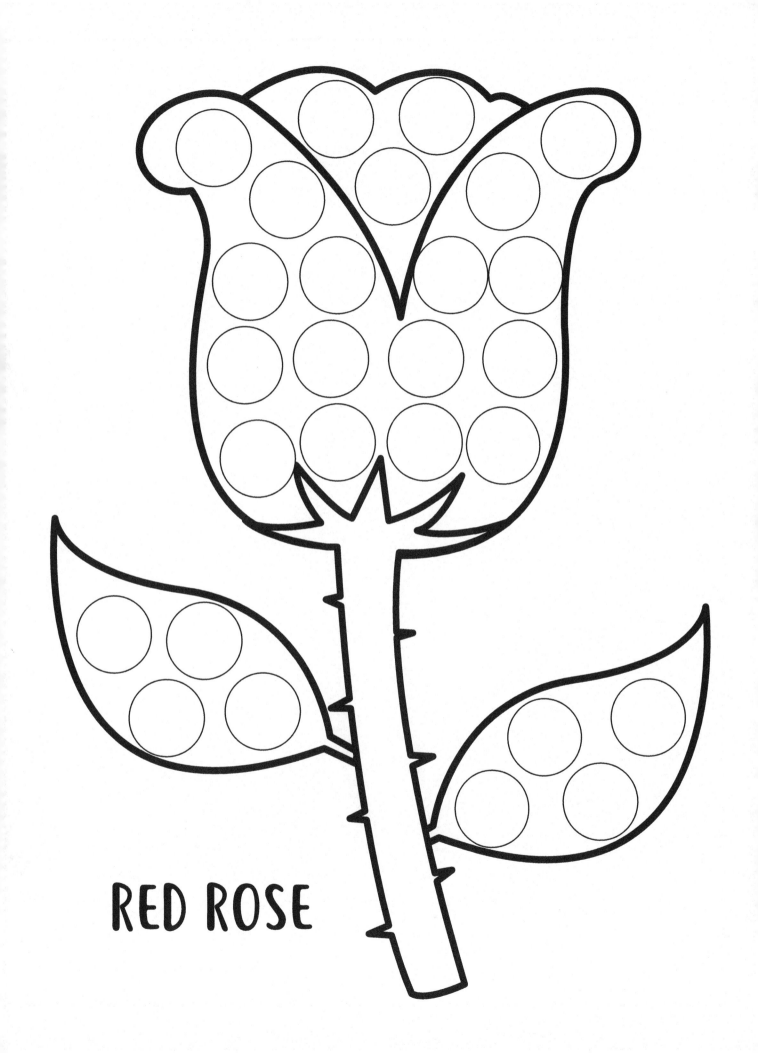

RED ROSE

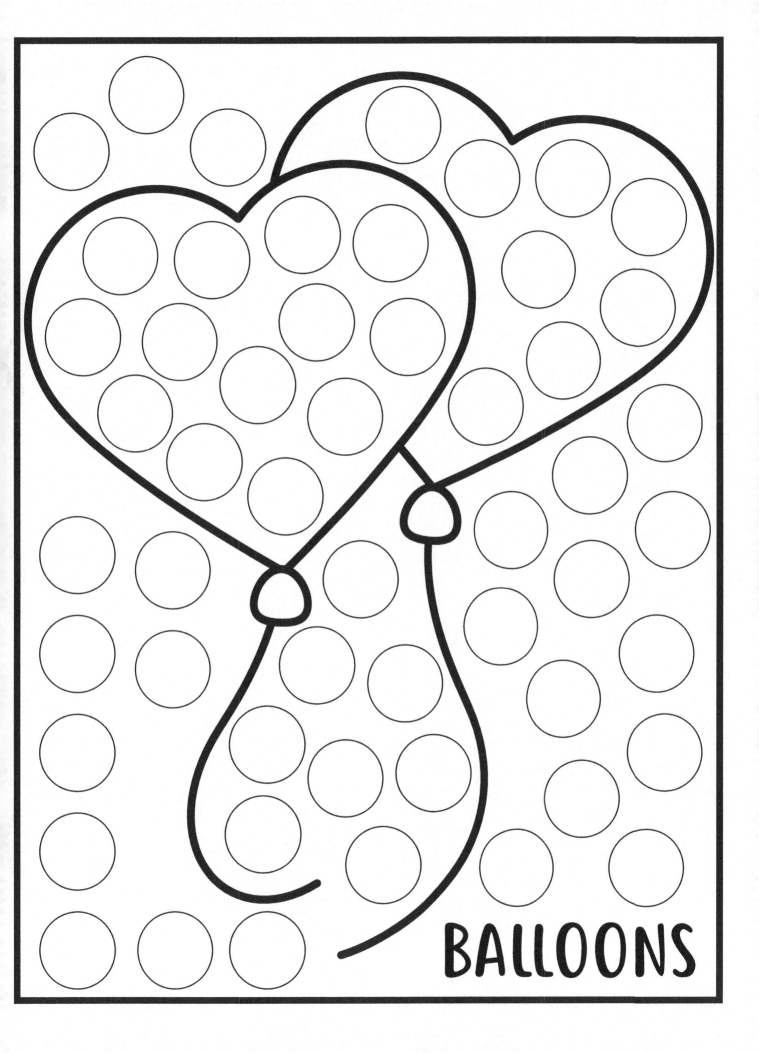

BALLOONS

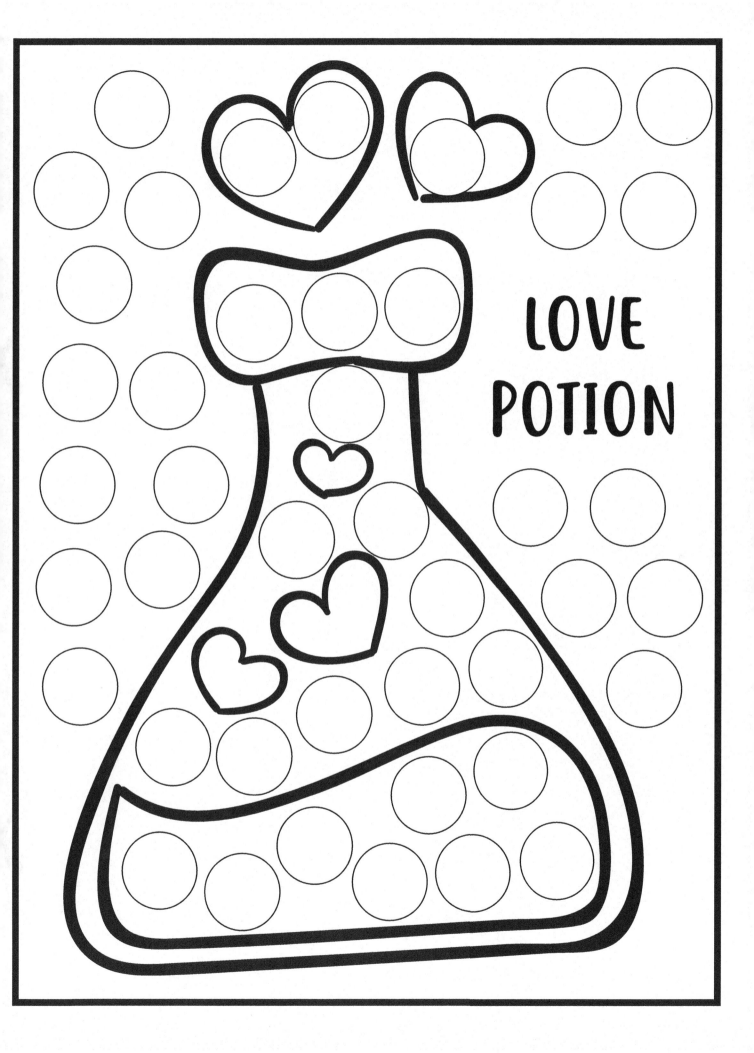

CANDLELIGHT DINNER

HOT-AIR BALLOON

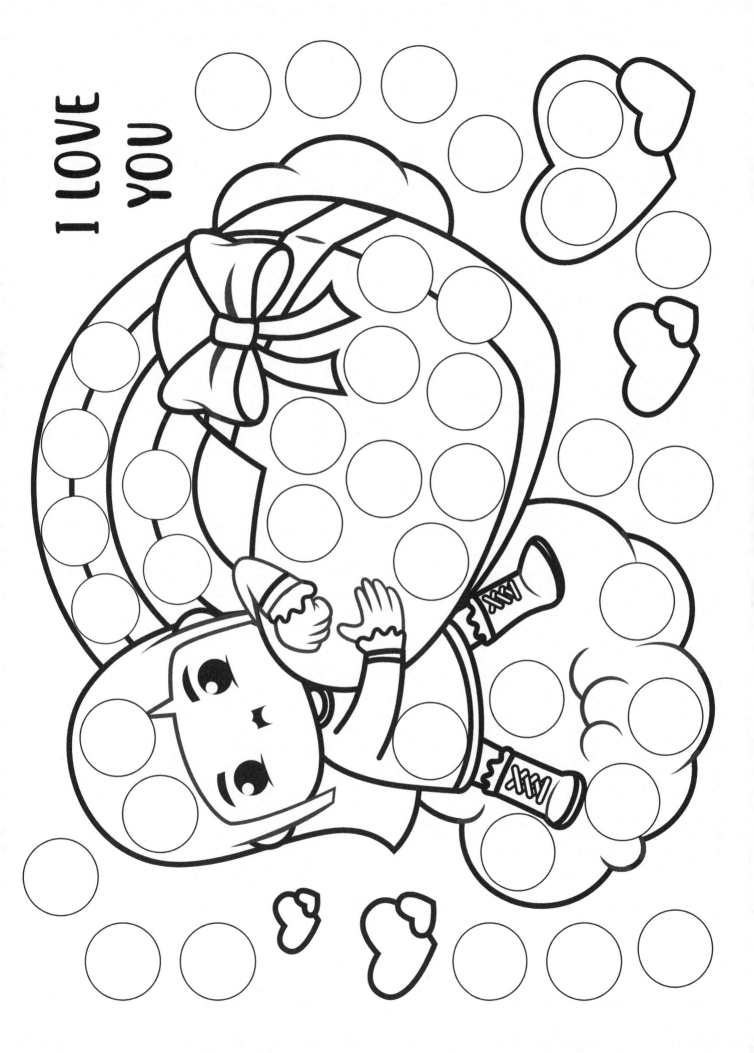

DID YOU ENJOY THIS BOOK?

Write us what you think
by scanning the QR code below

United States

Share some
PICTURES of your
ARTWORK with us
in your review!

If you bought this book **outside the United States**,
you can review it by scanning the codes below.

Canada

Australia

UK

LOTS OF AWESOME DOT MARKERS BOOKS ARE WAITING FOR YOU!

Scan the qr code to discover them.

Dinosaurs

Unicorns

Sea Life
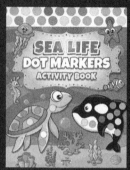

Vehicles

Easter

Mother's Day
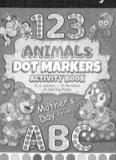

Summer

4th of July

Animals ABC

Halloween

Thanksgiving

Christmas

Christmas ABC

Hanukkah

and many more...!!!

KINDRELL
Land Press

FOLLOW US ON

@kindrelllandpress

@kindrelllandpress

@kindrelllandpress

amazon

Kindrell Land Press 🔍

Made in the USA
Las Vegas, NV
06 August 2023

75737519R00044